Insurrection!

How Afrikans Took Our Freedom Back

A Book to Free Young Black Minds

Angela Freeman

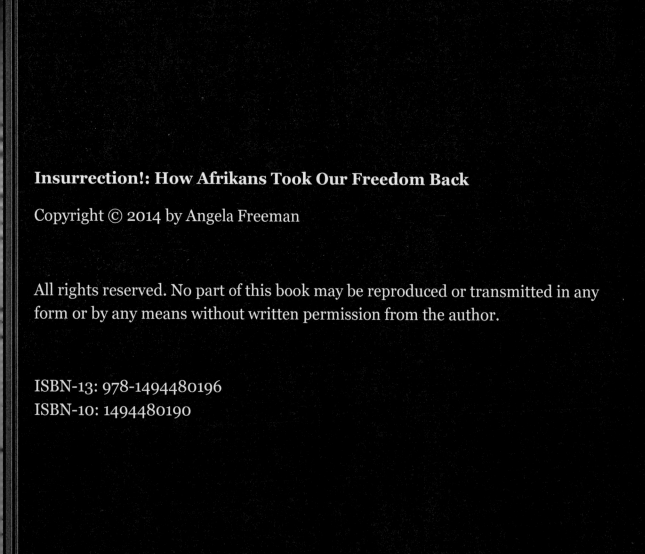

Insurrection!: How Afrikans Took Our Freedom Back

Copyright © 2014 by Angela Freeman

ISBN-13: 978-1494480196
ISBN-10: 1494480190

Dedication

This book is dedicated to precious Black children worldwide, not being taught how great they truly are. Demand respect! Never be afraid to stand up and fight for your race. Hold your heads up high.

Insurrection – fighting evil people in a war for freedom

Throughout history, villains from other races have threatened great Afrikan civilizations. They seek to destroy us and take our freedom. From time to time, an Afrikan Insurrection Leader is born who is destined to strike a mighty blow to our enemies. This book contains the accounts of a few great Afrikan Leaders that guided us to freedom through insurrection!

In the beginning, Afrikans lived in great civilizations filled with peace, love, and harmony. The men protected the women and the women took care of their families. Children loved and respected their parents. They grew up to be healthy, strong, and wise.

Afrikans were very rich. We had plenty of farmland, gold and diamond mines, universities, and castles. There were lots of beautiful markets selling fine clothes, colorful jewelry, and delicious food. Afrikans had strong armies filled with fierce warrior men and women. We enjoyed peaceful, happy lives.

One day, a group of white savages invaded Afrika. They tricked innocent Black people, and then kidnapped us from our homes and families. The savages put us Afrikans in chains and threw us on boats.

The ships were overcrowded. There was no room to move. It was hard to breath. The ships were filthy and the germs caused many Afrikans to get sick or die. They brought us Afrikans to a faraway land called the Americas.

In the Americas, the white savages were very mean to Afrikans. They enslaved us - that means they took away our freedom. The whites frequently beat, whipped, and killed Afrikans. They forced us to eat pork and other bad foods that made us sick.

Afrikans were required to do very hard work from before sunrise in the morning until after sunset at night. We didn't get breaks or a paycheck. There were bad men called "overseers" who would torture us if we didn't work fast enough.

Usually the overseers were whites. They abused Afrikans by striking us with whips. We called the white savages "crackers" or "cracker man" because of the "cracking" noise their whips made while cutting into our flesh. Sometimes the wicked white savages forced Afrikans to hurt other Afrikans.

Afrikans were enslaved in the U.S.A. and in other countries such as Ayiti (Haiti), Jamaica, Brazil, and Mexico. Afrikans did not want to be slaves. We decided to fight back!

The Afrikans living in the country of Ayiti decided to fight for their freedom. A Vodun priest, François Mackandal, was one of the first insurrection leaders in Ayiti. After several years of combat, he was captured. We needed a new leader to continue our fight for liberation.

In Afrikan culture, we perform spiritual ceremonies and consult the ancestors before making important decisions. The Afrikans held a sacred Vodun ceremony to choose the new leader. The priestess Cecile Fatiman lead a ceremony in which a priest named Boukman Dutty was chosen to lead the insurrection. They performed sacred rituals and took a divine oath to liberate our people.

Boukman was a strong warrior. He was born in a country called Jamaica before being brought to Ayiti by enslavers. He believed all of the evil white savages had to leave Ayiti or they must be killed. Boukman would not consider sharing Ayiti with the savages because they only wanted to hurt Afrikans and make us suffer. He knew that if we let them live, they would continue to oppress us. Afrikans can never live in peace with white savages.

Afrikan women played an important role in the Ayiti insurrection. Because the enslaver's women were useless (*they didn't cook, clean, or nurse their own babies*), the savages thought all women were too dumb to pose a threat. They underestimated the power of strong Afrikan women.

Afrikan women always played a major role in our battles. They helped Afrikan men win wars against our enemies; even if the male warriors got killed they kept fighting. Afrikan women are our secret weapon.

Boukman was very wise. He knew that many Afrikan women were forced to be maids and cooks for whites. He asked these women to help the revolt by poisoning the enslaver's food when the time was right.

When Boukman was ready to start the insurrection, the Afrikan women across Ayiti poisoned the food of their enslavers. The savages became too sick and weak to fight, and many of them died. We began this insurrection on **August 22, 1791**.

The Afrikan warriors stormed in and began killing the savages. They slit the throats of over 1,000 enslavers. Boukman's Army put the heads of dead whites on sticks as souvenirs of the revolution. The Afrikans set fire to the savage's homes, plantations, and businesses. Cities were engulfed with flames and smoke as Ayiti burned.

The Afrikans continued to fight courageously under Boukman's leadership. They refused to remain enslaved to the evil whites. These strong Afrikan warriors understood that all righteous men are willing to die to protect their people. Our brave brother Boukman Dutty was killed during one of the battles. However, his spirit lived on in the hearts of the Afrikan warriors in Ayiti!

After the mighty leader Boukman transitioned, the Afrikans of Ayiti needed a new leader. After trying a few different men, they chose a man named Toussaint L'Overtuer. Toussaint was a wise military man, but there was one problem.

Before the insurrection, Toussaint became wealthy by profiting from the enslavement of his own Afrikan Brothers and Sisters. His goal was to ensure the Afrikans weren't badly hurt during slavery, but he didn't want the Afrikans to stop working on plantations. Toussaint wanted to get along with the savages so he could keep making money from the Afrikans' servitude.

Toussaint led the Afrikan troops in many successful battles against the savages. He would always be nice to any whites he captured as prisoners. Toussaint wanted to impress the savage enslavers by being merciful. He didn't realize whites don't respect mercy. Unlike Toussaint, the savages would brutally torture any Afrikans they captured.

Toussaint was a talented soldier, but he didn't understand that whites are the natural enemies of Afrikans. He was more interested in winning our enemies' respect and praise than liberating our suffering people. Toussaint fought bravely, but for the wrong reasons.

One day, the whites tricked Toussaint into surrendering. They kidnapped him and took him to a faraway country of savages called France. Even though Toussaint had always been very kind to all white prisoners in Ayiti, when the savages captured him, they tortured him and let him starve to death in jail.

Meanwhile, Toussaint's General, Jean-Jacques Dessalines, took power. Unlike Toussaint, Dessalines was completely loyal to Afrikan people. He wanted to see all Afrikans free by any means necessary.

Dessalines was much tougher than Toussaint. He believed in "an atrocity for an atrocity". Every time the enslavers killed an Afrikan, his army would kill whites without mercy or remorse.

Dessalines was wise and uncompromising, like his ancestor Boukman Dutty. He was not afraid to be extremely violent to free his people. Dessalines was a shining example of strong Black manhood. He understood that vengeance against evil was a righteous obligation.

Often, the enslavers forced Afrikan women to have babies with them. This created a lot of mulattoes (*mixed race people*) in Ayiti. The whites didn't really love their mulatto children, but they treated them better than the Afrikans.

This special treatment made many of the mulattoes think they were superior to the full-blooded Afrikans. Often, their white fathers would send the mulattoes to school, provide them with good jobs, and give them land. These benefits made the mulattoes wealthy and powerful. Because of this, most of the mulattoes were loyal to their white fathers and betrayed their enslaved Afrikan mothers.

Some of the mixed race people enslaved Afrikans. Other mixed race people chose to fight on the righteous Afrikan side. However, most mulattos fought with the white savages in battles against Afrikans. One day those mulattoes realized uniting with whites wasn't a good idea.

After years of fighting the Afrikans in Ayiti, the enslavers sent their most wicked General, a savage beast named Rochambeau, to seize control of Ayiti from the Afrikans. Rochambeau was brutal. He loved killing and hated everyone who wasn't white.

One day, Rochambeau invited the wives of the mulatto Generals to a fancy dinner party. They had lots of fun while dancing and eating fine foods. At the end of the night Rochambeau had gifts for each of the wives. The whites brought out beautifully wrapped boxes. When the mulatto wives opened the boxes they found the severed heads of their husbands. Rochambeau wanted to be sure they understood that he would kill mulattoes just like he killed Afrikans.

This gruesome gift was a shock to the mulattos of Ayiti. They decided to join forces with the Afrikans to protect themselves from the wrath of the Rochambeau and his white army.

During the revolution in Ayiti, the French savages spent all of their money trying to defeat the Afrikans in war. At that time, the savage enslavers owned a large area of land in North America. They called it the Louisiana Territory. The savages decided to sell the land very cheaply to the United States. They were in desperate need of more money to fund the war.

This deal doubled the size of the U.S.A. In fact, if it wasn't for the insurrection in Ayiti, the U.S.A. would not include the states now known as Louisiana, Missouri, Arkansas, Iowa, Minnesota, Nebraska, Colorado, North Dakota, South Dakota, Wyoming, and Oklahoma. The white savages of France lost it all because of the power of Dessalines and the Afrikans of Ayiti!

Shortly after the whites sold the Louisiana Territory, the Afrikans in Ayiti declared victory and began kicking the savages out of the land. After the insurrection, some Afrikans began feeling sorry for the whites that were still on the island. They knew Dessalines was going to kill them all. These foolish Afrikans helped the whites hide from Dessalines and the freedom fighters.

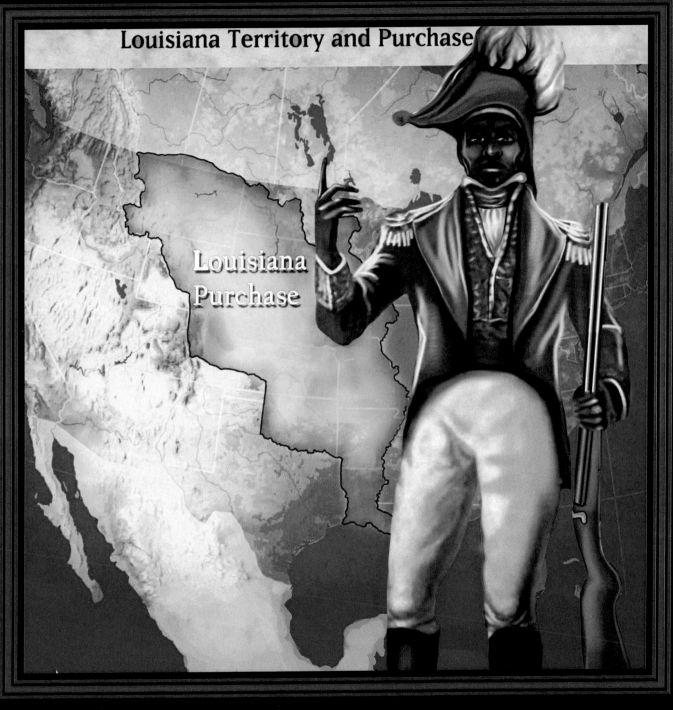

Louisiana
Purchase

Dessalines had a brilliant plan to finally get rid of the evil savages – once and for all! He spread the word that every white that came out of hiding would be forgiven, but if they kept hiding they would eventually be killed. The Afrikan race-traitors who helped the enslavers warned them to stay in hiding, but the savages didn't listen.

Dessalines threw a splendid party and foolish whites came from all over Ayiti. They laughed, ate, and celebrated late into the night. At the end of the festivities, Dessalines' army opened fire on the savages, killing them.

After liberating Ayiti in 1804, the Afrikans knew there was still work to do. There were Afrikans in many other countries that needed help liberating themselves!

The brave leaders of Ayiti began a plan to join forces with Afrikans throughout the Americas and have an even bigger insurrection! Enslaved Afrikans were inspired by the Ayiti Revolution. The fight for independence was on!

Gabriel Prosser was an enslaved Afrikan in the state of Virginia. He was a blacksmith and was often sent to different places to work. While traveling, Gabriel heard Afrikans talking about the great insurrection happening in Ayiti. He was inspired to begin planning his own insurrection with other Afrikans in the U.S.A. Soon, Gabriel's troops were ready to begin fighting, but he was forced to wait because of bad weather.

While the Afrikans waited to start their revolt, two of them got scared. The cowards told the white enslavers about the planned insurrection. The whites quickly brought in their army to stop the revolt, but Gabriel managed to escape. The whites offered a $300 reward for help capturing Gabriel. A cowardly, selfish Black race-traitor told the whites where to find Gabriel. The traitor wanted the money to buy his own freedom. He didn't care about the other enslaved Afrikans. The whites captured Gabriel and the other Afrikans who helped plan the rebellion. The savages only paid the race-traitor $50.

Slavery remained legal, but the whites were petrified!

Denmark Vesey was an enslaved Afrikan in the state of South Carolina. Denmark had lived in several different countries, including Ayiti. One day, Denmark won the lottery and was able to purchase his freedom.

Afrikans in the U.S.A. were greatly inspired by the liberation of Ayiti. As a result, the revolutionary spirit within Denmark began to grow. Denmark's freedom was not enough. He wanted freedom for all enslaved Afrikans! Denmark and his partners planned to exterminate all the white enslavers in the city of Charleston, South Carolina. Then, they would travel to Florida to join forces with a group of Afrikans and Indigenous people called the Seminoles. Finally, they would join with the Afrikan army from Ayiti to free all Afrikans in the U.S.A from slavery.

Word spread far and wide in the Afrikan community that freedom was on the way. Unfortunately, two cowardly Black race-traitors betrayed our people. They told the white savages about the planned insurrection. The savages murdered Denmark and most of his followers.

Slavery remained legal, but the whites were terrified!

In the event that he was killed, or his insurrection wasn't completely successful, Denmark Vesey planned to make sure some of his students survived. Before the revolution, he sent them away to other states. His students were instructed to continue the fight, even if Denmark was captured.

One student's name was David Walker. David Walker was born free. He hated slavery and wanted all Afrikans to be liberated. Walker was an excellent writer.

After Denmark Vesey was captured by white savages, David Walker began writing an appeal to Afrikans. He told us to take our freedom by any means necessary. David knew the white savages would never do anything good for Afrikans, so we had to take action.

David Walker's Appeal was spread far and wide across the U.S.A. It inspired many Afrikans to prepare for revolution.

Nat Turner was an enslaved Afrikan in Southampton County, Virginia. He was a very special man. He often had divine visions of how to free Afrikans from slavery. Nat was inspired by Afrikans before him such as David Walker, Denmark Vesey, Gabriel Prosser, Queen Nanny of Jamaica, The Gullah Nation, Jean-Jacques Dessalines, and Boukman Dutty. Because of his visions, many Afrikans believed Nat was a prophet from God.

One day, God revealed to Nat Turner, "In order to get free, you must exterminate the enslavers." Nat gathered a group of enslaved Afrikan Warriors. When the time was right, on **August 21, 1831**, they began freeing Afrikans. Nat Turner's righteous troops killed the white oppressors including men, women, and children in the name of Black liberation.

Whites can't stop Afrikans unless the traitors among us help them. Our unity is powerful. If one of us doesn't succeed in gaining complete liberation, another Afrikan will build upon our works until the mission is accomplished. Nat Turner perfected the work of those liberators who came before him.

35

The Prophet Nat Turner scared our enemies so much, many cowardly savages in Virginia wanted to end slavery right away. They were afraid of more insurrections. The vote to end slavery was close, but slavery remained intact for a while. Shortly after, in 1865, the government of the United States decided to spare the lives of American enslavers by ending chattel slavery. Otherwise, the savages would have faced many more bloody insurrections!

After Afrikans forcefully took our freedom through insurrection, we began building rich communities like the ones we had in Afrika. Some of the rich communities we built were Rosewood, Florida; Greenwood in Tulsa, Oklahoma; Jackson Ward in Richmond, Virginia; and Durham, North Carolina.

The evil white savages never stopped trying to destroy Afrikan communities. Today, they use advanced warfare strategies such as mis-education, drugs, politics, crime, economics, and media. It is your responsibility to become a great leader for your race. Afrikans must continue to fight our oppressors until the very end. Our survival depends on it.

Who is the next Afrikan Insurrection Leader?

YOU!

Our ancestors live on through us! We have a divine duty to study and work hard to free Black people worldwide. Our Afrikan Insurrection Leaders sacrificed for us to continue the fight for liberation. Don't let them down. You have the power!

The Haitian Revolution Prayer

"Great God who created the Earth; who created the sun that gives us light. The God who holds up the ocean; who makes the thunder roar. Our God who has ears to hear: Although you are hidden in the clouds; you watch us from where you are. You see all that the whites have made us suffer.

The white man's god commands him to commit crimes and acts of evil. But our God commands us to do good. Our God, who is so Good, and believes in justice, He orders us to avenge wrongs committed against us. It is He who will direct our arms and walk with us into victory. It is He who will assist us. We must throw away the image of the white man's god who has so often brought us misery, and listen to the voice for liberty that sings in all our hearts."

Boukman Dutty of Ayiti – August 22, 1791

Black Books For Black Children

  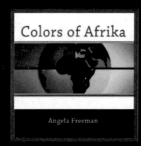 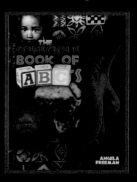

For More Information visit **www.authorangelafreeman.com**

The first to the mind wins!